# WELCOME TO THE WORLD OF INFOGRAPHICS

Using icons, graphics and pictograms, infographics visualise data and information in a whole new way!

**BE AMAZED BY THE REAL-LIFE SIZE OF THE WORLD'S LARGEST SPIDER**

**DISCOVER WHICH ANIMAL CAN JUMP THE EQUIVALENT OF A HUMAN LEAPING OVER A SKYSCRAPER!**

**FIND OUT WHICH ANIMAL WOULD WIN THE GOLD MEDAL IN A SPRINT RACE**

**MEASURE THE LENGTH OF A BLUE WHALE IN BUSES, PEOPLE AND BASKETBALL COURTS**

# ORDER OF LIVING THINGS

Our planet is teeming with billions of organisms, from microscopic algae to gigantic whales. In order to identify each living thing, scientists use a classification system.

## KINGDOMS

**ANIMALS**

**PLANTS**

**FUNGI**

**PROTISTS**
(MICRO-ORGANISMS)

**EUBACTERIA**
(MICRO-ORGANISMS)

**ARCHEOBACTERIA**
(MICRO-ORGANISMS)

### CLASSIFICATION
All living things belong to one of six kingdoms. Each kingdom is divided into groups, from phylum down to species. The graphic shows how a species, in this case the wolf, is identified using this classification system.

INSECTS OUTNUMBER HUMANS BY

## 200,000,000 TO 1

**PHYLUM**
*CHORDATA*
Animals with backbones

**CLASS**
*MAMMALIA*
Mammals

**ORDER**
*CARNIVORA*
Meat-eating mammals

**FAMILY**
*CANIDAE*
Foxes, dogs and wolves

SO FAR, SOME
# 5,500
SPECIES OF
MAMMALS HAVE
BEEN IDENTIFIED
AND NAMED.

**GENUS**
*CANIS*
Dogs and wolves

**SPECIES**
*CANIS LUPUS*
Wolf

5

# MICROSCOPIC WORLD

There are entire kingdoms of micro-organisms that are too small to see with the naked eye. For example, a single gram of soil can contain 40 million bacteria alone!

### BIGGEST KILLERS
The number of people killed each year by various diseases caused by micro-organisms.

## 3.9 MILLION
LOWER RESPIRATORY INFECTIONS (SUCH AS PNEUMONIA)

## 2.8 MILLION
HIV/AIDS

## 1.8 MILLION
DIARRHEAL DISEASES

**1.6 MILLION**
TB

**1.3 MILLION**
MALARIA

**0.6 MILLION**
MEASLES

### BREAD
Not all micro-organisms are harmful. Humans use some in food and drink and to treat waste. For example, yeast is used in bread-making to turn the sugars in bread dough into tiny bubbles of carbon dioxide, making the bread 'rise'.

## 400 NANOMETRES
The size of the largest viruses – about 1/250th the width of a human hair.

FLAGELLA

## CELLS

All organisms are made up of cells. Micro-organisms often consist of one cell, while plants and animals are made up of billions. Prokaryotic cells are those that do not contain a cell nucleus. They include bacteria, some of which have flagella, which they wiggle to move about.

NUCLEUS

NUCLEUS

**PLANT CELL**

## EUKARYOTIC

Eukaryotic cells contain a cell nucleus, inside which is the genetic information for the cell. Plants and animals are formed from two different types of eukaryotic cells.

**ANIMAL CELL**

About 10,000 human cells could fit onto the head of a pin

# 10,000

## THE LARGEST KNOWN CELLS ARE UNFERTILISED OSTRICH EGGS.

They weigh about 1.6 kg – nearly two bags of sugar.

**CHICKEN EGG**

**ALLIGATOR EGG**

**TURTLE EGG**

**HUMMINGBIRD EGG**

# ENERGY PRODUCTION

The Sun is the source of most of the energy used on our planet. Plants convert this energy into substances that all living things can then use to produce energy to survive and grow.

**LIGHT ENERGY FROM THE SUN**

**CHLOROPHYLL**

**WATER**

**CARBON DIOXIDE**

## PHOTOSYNTHESIS

Chlorophyll is found inside many plant cells. It plays an important part in harnessing sunlight during a process called photosynthesis. This process converts water and the gas carbon dioxide into sugars and oxygen.

## WITH OR WITHOUT

Respiration that uses oxygen is called aerobic, while respiration that does not use oxygen is called anaerobic.

**OXYGEN**

**SUGAR**

EACH YEAR, ONE HECTARE OF TREES CONSUMES THE SAME AMOUNT OF CARBON DIOXIDE PRODUCED BY AN AVERAGE CAR THAT HAS BEEN DRIVEN FOR

# 100,000 KM

That same hectare of trees also produces enough oxygen for

## RESPIRATION

During respiration, sugars are used to produce energy. Tiny structures called mitochondria found in cells are the main sites for this energy production. As well as producing energy, this process also creates the gas carbon dioxide and water.

**MITOCHONDRIA**

# 45

people to breathe for a year.

# GENES AND CELL DIVISION

Every organism contains instructions that determine how it looks and behaves. These instructions are stored on a long, twisted molecule called DNA.

BASE PAIR

CYTOSINE    GUANINE

ADENINE    THYMINE

PHOSPHATE BACKBONE

## DNA MOLECULE

A DNA molecule consists of two twisting backbones, which are joined together by chemicals that are linked in pairs, called base pairs. These pairs are organised into certain sequences, called genes, and these determine how an organism acts.

There are an estimated 3 billion DNA bases in the human genome

# 3,000,000,000

## CHROMOSOMES

Chromosomes are structures found inside cells. They are made up of long strands of DNA that are twisted and coiled together tightly.

If it was unravelled, the **DNA** from a single **cell** in a **human body** would be approximately **2 metres** long – that's taller than most humans!

## CELL DIVISION

Cells divide in order to multiply. To do this, they need to duplicate their genetic information before splitting apart.

HUMANS AND CHIMPS SHARE UP TO

**95%**

OF THEIR DNA

**1.** PARENT CELL

**2.** NUCLEUS DIVIDES

**3.** CELL SPLITS

**4.** TWO DAUGHTER CELLS

# REPRODUCTION

All living things reproduce, so that their species can survive. Reproduction can be asexual, whereby one organism duplicates itself, or sexual, whereby cells from two organisms join together to produce young.

BUD

## ASEXUAL REPRODUCTION

Some simple organisms, such as amoeba, will simply divide in two. Others, such as this hydra, reproduce by budding, creating an identical, but smaller, version of themselves.

## FLOWERS AND SEEDS

Plants contain male cells, called pollen, stored in anthers, and female cells inside an ovary. The two cells join together to form seeds. Some seeds, such as the pips in an apple, are surrounded by fruit. Animals eat the fruit and the seeds are spread in the animals' dung. Sycamore seeds have a special wing shape, which allows them to spin away from the parent plant and spread.

PETAL

STIGMA

ANTHER

STYLE

SEED WINGS

**SYCAMORE SEEDS**

FILAMENT

OVARY

**APPLE SEEDS**

FRUIT

THIN ALBUMEN

THICK ALBUMEN

YOLK

DEVELOPING EMBRYO

SHELL

AIR CELL

## LAYING EGGS

Many animals lay eggs which contain the developing young. Inside a chicken's egg, the developing young, or embryo, is fed by nutrients in the yolk, while being supported and protected by the albumen.

## LIVE BIRTH

The young of mammals develop inside the mother's uterus. This development period is called the gestation. Over time, the young will develop and grow until they are old enough to be born.

FEMALE ELEPHANT **3,000 KG**

# 22 MONTHS

GESTATION PERIOD FOR AN ELEPHANT – THE LONGEST OF ANY LAND ANIMAL.

CALF 105 KG

RABBITS HAVE A FAST BREEDING RATE. IN A SINGLE BREEDING SEASON, A PAIR CAN MULTIPLY TO AS MANY AS

# 800

RABBITS OVER THREE OR FOUR GENERATIONS.

# GROWING UP

As a plant or animal gets older, it grows and matures before it finally dies. During its life span, it may go through many stages, including a complete change in body shape and form.

## HOW LONG CAN ANIMALS LIVE?

ANT 6 MONTHS

MOUSE
4 YEARS

RABBIT
10 YEARS

## LIFE CYCLES

Some animals, including butterflies, change completely as they mature. This process is called metamorphosis. Mammals, such as horses, keep the same body shape, but grow larger.

SPROUT

SEED

SAPLING

MATURE TREE

CATERPILLAR

PUPA

EGGS

BUTTERFLY

A **Great Basin Bristlecone pine** in North America is the **oldest** known living individual tree. Samples from its core and rings show that it is more than **4,800 years old.**

**BOTTLENOSE DOLPHIN**
45 YEARS

**HORSE**
30 YEARS

**KOI CARP**
70 YEARS

**ASIAN ELEPHANT**
60 YEARS

**HUMAN**
70–80 YEARS

**GALAPAGOS TORTOISE**
190 YEARS

**YEARLING**

**HORSE**

**FOAL**

# 4,265

A type of black coral called Leiopathes is one of the oldest continuously living organisms. Some specimens of the coral are around 4,265 years old.

# FOOD WEBS

Most energy comes from the Sun. This energy is harnessed by plants and passed on when they are eaten by animals, who are, in turn, eaten by their predators. This relationship is called a food chain.

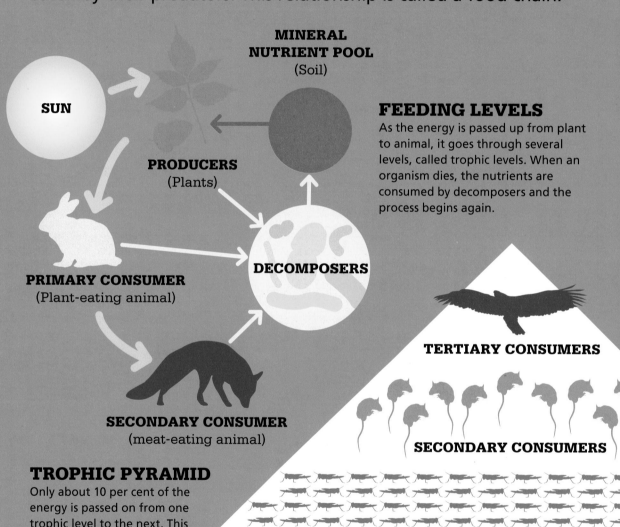

**MINERAL NUTRIENT POOL**
(Soil)

**SUN**

**PRODUCERS**
(Plants)

**DECOMPOSERS**

**PRIMARY CONSUMER**
(Plant-eating animal)

**SECONDARY CONSUMER**
(meat-eating animal)

## FEEDING LEVELS
As the energy is passed up from plant to animal, it goes through several levels, called trophic levels. When an organism dies, the nutrients are consumed by decomposers and the process begins again.

**TERTIARY CONSUMERS**

**SECONDARY CONSUMERS**

**PRIMARY CONSUMERS**

**PRODUCERS**

## TROPHIC PYRAMID
Only about 10 per cent of the energy is passed on from one trophic level to the next. This means that there are fewer living things the higher up the trophic levels you go, creating a trophic pyramid.

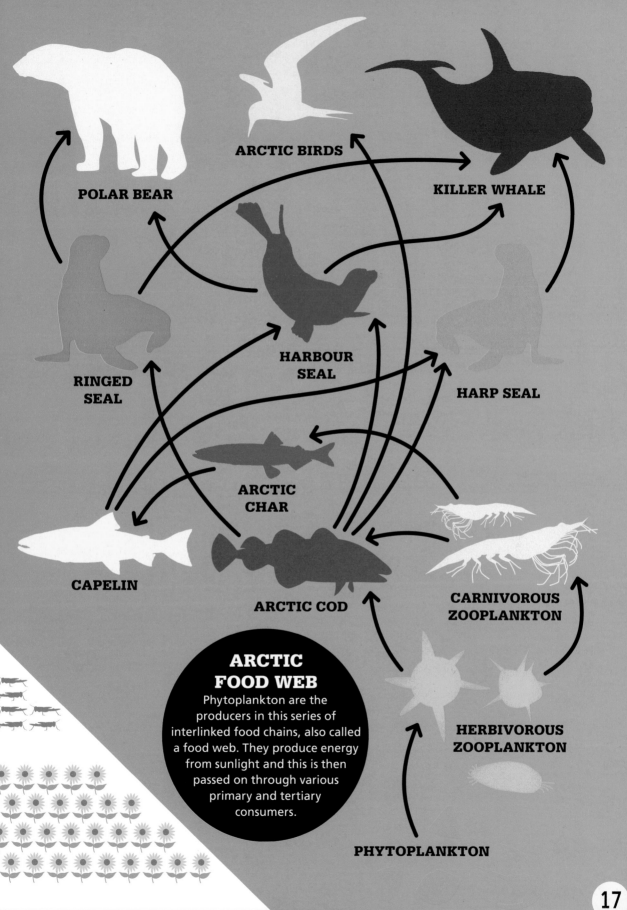

POLAR BEAR

ARCTIC BIRDS

KILLER WHALE

RINGED SEAL

HARBOUR SEAL

HARP SEAL

ARCTIC CHAR

CAPELIN

ARCTIC COD

CARNIVOROUS ZOOPLANKTON

## ARCTIC FOOD WEB

Phytoplankton are the producers in this series of interlinked food chains, also called a food web. They produce energy from sunlight and this is then passed on through various primary and tertiary consumers.

HERBIVOROUS ZOOPLANKTON

PHYTOPLANKTON

# EVOLUTION

Throughout the history of the Earth, new species have appeared while others have died out or changed. This process is called evolution and it occurs in response to changing conditions on our planet.

**98%**

2%

1800

**95%**

5%

1900

## MOTH

The peppered moth has changed as its habitat has altered. During the 19th century, pollution from factories darkened tree barks. This meant that light versions of the moth were easy to spot by predators. Dark varieties made up a tiny amount of peppered moths at the start of the 19th century. By 1900, they made up more than 95 per cent.

## EXTINCTION

When a species dies out it becomes extinct. There have been several periods when a lot of species died out – these are called mass extinction events. This graphic shows rates of species extinction – the taller the peak the more species died out. Mass extinctions have a wide range of causes, including massive volcanic activity, sudden climate change and asteroid impacts.

ORDOVICIAN–SILURIAN
EXTINCTION EVENT
**450 MYA**

LATE DEVONIA
EXTINCTION
EVENT
**374 MYA**

% OF SPECIES EXTINCTION

100%
90%
80%
70%
60%
50%
40%
30%
20%
10%

MILLIONS OF
YEARS AGO (MYA)

500      450      400      350

# FINCHES

British scientist Charles Darwin developed the theory of evolution by studying animal life on the Galapagos Islands in the Pacific. Here, he noticed that various species of finches had differently shaped beaks to suit the types of food they ate.

| FRUIT EATERS | INSECT EATERS | | | | | CACTUS EATERS | SEED EATERS | | |
|---|---|---|---|---|---|---|---|---|---|
| PARROT BEAK | GRASPING BEAKS | | PROBING BEAKS | | | | CRUSHING BEAKS | | |
| VEGETARIAN TREE FINCH | LARGE TREE FINCH | SMALL TREE FINCH | WOODPECKER FINCH | WARBLER FINCH | CACTUS FINCH | SMALL GROUND FINCH | MEDIUM GROUND FINCH | LARGE GROUND FINCH |
| TREE FINCHES | | | | WARBLER FINCHES | GROUND FINCHES | | | |

**PERMIAN–TRIASSIC** EXTINCTION EVENT **252.28 MYA**

**TRIASSIC–JURASSIC** EXTINCTION EVENT **199.6 MYA**

During the extinction event at the Permian-Triassic **96%** of all marine species and **70%** of all land species died out.

**CRETACEOUS–TERTIARY** EXTINCTION EVENT **65.5 MYA**

250    200    150    100    50    0

# FAST AND SLOW

Living beings often use speed for survival, for example to outrun a predator. Other organisms live at a slower pace in order to save energy.

The fastest accelerating living thing on the planet is the hat thrower fungus. The spores are released on a jet of liquid with an acceleration of

## 0–32 KM/H IN JUST 2 MILLIONTHS OF A SECOND

experiencing forces of 20,000G – astronauts blasting into space only experience 4G.

## FASTEST ANIMALS

**PEREGRINE FALCON**
320 KM/H

**SPEED**

## AUSTRALIAN TIGER BEETLES

CAN REACH SPEEDS OF 6.7 KM/H WHEN ESCAPING PREDATORS. BUT THEY ARE ONLY 1 CM LONG, SO THEY TRAVEL AT ABOUT

### 170 BODY LENGTHS PER SECOND.

IF AN OLYMPIC SPRINTER COULD MATCH THAT RATE OF BODY LENGTHS PER SECOND, THEY WOULD BE RUNNING AT NEARLY

# 1,200 KM/H

– THAT'S FASTER THAN THE SPEED OF SOUND AT SEA LEVEL!

# SLOWEST ANIMALS

**GIANT TORTOISE**
0.3 KM/H

**GARDEN SNAIL**
0.03 KM/H

**IN ONE MINUTE A GARDEN SNAIL CAN TRAVEL**

**5 CM**

**SEAHORSE**
0.02 KM/H

**IN ONE HOUR THEY CAN GROW**
**4 CM**

Some species of bamboo are the fastest growing plants in the world, capable of growing 1 metre in a single day

**SWORDFISH AND MARLIN**
100 KM/H
**FASTEST FISH**

**HORSE**
70 KM/H

**HUMAN SPRINTER**
37.5 KM/H

**CHEETAH** 120 KM/H
**FASTEST LAND ANIMAL**

**WOLF** 65 KM/H

AT THIS SPEED, THE AUSTRALIAN TIGER BEETLE WOULD COMPLETE 100 METRES IN JUST

# 0.3 SECONDS.

AN OLYMPIC SPRINTER TAKES
10 SECONDS TO RUN 100 METRES.

# BIG AND SMALL

Whether they reach super-size proportions or can pass through the eye of a needle, these record-breaking organisms have found their own way of surviving in the world.

A **giant fungus** of the honey mushroom species covers **8.9 sq km** of land in Oregon, USA, making it the **largest** ever known organism by area.

GIRAFFE
6 M

Standing next to some of the tallest animals in the world, the average human is a little short. Top of the tree are giraffes, which can reach more than three times an average person's height.

OSTRICH 2.75 M

ELEPHANT **4 M**

MAN
1.8 M

HORSE
2.2 M

# THE BLUE WHALE IS THE LARGEST ANIMAL EVER

## IT CAN WEIGH UP TO
# 200 TONNES
ABOUT THE WEIGHT OF 40 ELEPHANTS, OR 15 BUSES.

# 30 M LONG
Which is about the same length as 17 people, 3 school buses or a basketball court.

It can eat up to four tonnes of krill in a day.

## ITS TONGUE CAN WEIGH AS MUCH AS AN ELEPHANT.

A newborn blue whale puts on about 90 kg of weight every single day during its first year.

## SMALLEST FLOWERING PLANT
### GENUS WOLFFIA
An individual plant is just 0.6 mm long and 0.3 mm wide.

ACTUAL SIZE

## BIGGEST FLOWER
### RAFFLESIA ARNOLDII
It measures up to 1 metre across and gives off an odour of decaying flesh.

CAMEL **2.15 M**

# Sequoia 115 m

# 29 Elephants

## TALLEST TREE

ACTUAL
SIZE

## GREATEST JUMPER

The froghopper is the world's greatest jumper. It can leap 70 cm into the air, but it's only 0.6 cm long.

THAT IS THE SAME AS A PERSON LEAPING OVER A 210-METRE HIGH SKYSCRAPER!

# RECORD BREAKERS

The creatures on these pages have developed some amazing ways of surviving, whether it is super-strength, deep-sea diving or living together in enormous groups.

## STRONGEST

Gram for gram, the world's strongest creature is thought to be the rhinoceros beetle. It can lift 850 times its own body weight.

That's equivalent to a human lifting

## 60 TONNES!

### ANT FACTS

In the Brazilian rainforest, the biomass of ants is roughly four times greater than that of all of the land vertebrates in the rainforest combined.

Although ants make up 2 per cent of all known insect species, they form at least one-third of all insect biomass.

The largest known swarm of locusts was made up of 40 billion insects and covered 1,036 square kilometres – that's the same size as the island of Tahiti.

# 40,000,000,000

The
**GOLIATH
BIRD-EATING
SPIDER**
has a leg span of up to

# 30 CM

and is the largest spider by mass.

HUMAN FREE
DIVER
273 м

EMPEROR
PENGUIN
500 м

LEATHERBACK
TURTLE
1,280 м

ELEPHANT SEAL
1,500 м

## DEEP DIVERS

**Argentine ants** live in enormous **mega-colonies**, one of which stretches for **6,000 km** along the Mediterranean Coast.

SPERM WHALE
3,000 м

FORMATION
OF EARTH
**4.5 BILLION
YEARS AGO**

# ANIMAL COUNTDOWN

Over billions of years, life on Earth has evolved from simple single-celled organisms into a wide range of complex creatures. On the way, new forms of life have appeared, while others have become extinct.

**1.5
BILLION
YEARS
AGO**

The Cambrian Explosion, about

**540 MYA** saw an enormous

expansion in life forms, including the

evolution of **chordates** (animals

with a backbone or notochord).

COMPLEX CELLS
**2 BILLION
YEARS AGO**

## Oldest fossils

The oldest fossils ever discovered were formed 3.4 billion years ago. They are the remains of ancient cells that lived at a time when the Earth was far warmer than today and its surface was covered with active volcanoes.

MULTICELLULAR LIFE
**1 BILLION YEARS AGO**

**3.5 BILLION YEARS AGO**

**3 BILLION YEARS AGO**

EVOLUTION OF PROKARYOTES
**3.8 BILLION YEARS AGO**

**2.5 BILLION YEARS AGO**

# 23:59

If the entire history of the Earth was condensed into just one single day, then modern humans would appear at one minute to midnight!

INSECTS
**400 MYA**

LAND PLANTS
**475 MYA**

FISH
**500 MYA**

REPTILES
**300 MYA**

MODERN HUMANS
**200,000 YEARS AGO**

MAMMALS
**200 MYA**

DINOSAURS DIED OUT
**65 MYA**

SIMPLE ANIMALS
**600 MILLION YEARS AGO (MYA)**

DINOSAURS
**245 MYA**

FLOWERS
**130 MYA**

**TODAY**

# UNDER THREAT

Today, many plant and animal species are threatened by the actions of one creature – humans. With their ability to change and destroy habitats, humans are pushing many species to extinction.

## 20%

The IUCN (International Union for Conservation of Nature) Red List from 2008 shows that about 1,140 of the 5,500 mammal species, or 20 per cent, are threatened with extinction.

## DEFORESTATION

At its peak in 1995, 29,000 square kilometres of the Amazon rainforest were being destroyed in a year – that's a rate of

# 3.3 SQ KM
# AN HOUR

or 80 square kilometres a day, which is bigger than the island of Manhattan, New York.

## WHALE DECLINE

The pre-whaling population of the blue whale was thought to be

# 350,000

Today there are
8–14,000

That's a fall of around
# 97%

## SAVE THE TIGER

Figures from 2011 show an increase in the tiger population from 1,411 in 2007 to 1,706. This rise is due to the protection of the tigers' core habitats.

2007
**1,411**

2011
**1,706**

## BORNEO DEFORESTATION

The area covered by rainforest on the island of Borneo (shown in green)

**1950**

**2010**

## ELEPHANT DECLINE

Elephant numbers in Chad have declined from

# 400,000
# IN 1970

TO
**10,000**
IN 2006

# GLOSSARY

## asexual reproduction

When something is able to create new versions of itself, or reproduce, without having to mate with another of its own species. Asexual reproduction can involve dividing or budding.

## bacteria

Tiny forms of life that are made up of one cell.

## biomass

The total amount of organisms in an area.

## cell

The fundamental building block of life. Cells are able to perform all of the functions that are essential for life, including producing energy and reproducing.

## consumer

An organism which feeds off other organisms that produce energy from sunlight.

## eukaryotic cell

A type of cell that contains several specific structures, including a nucleus, which holds the cell's genetic information.

## DNA

Short for deoxyribonucleic acid, this is the complex, twisting molecule found inside cells. It carries the genetic information that tells the cells how to perform.

## evolution

The process by which plants and animals change and adapt to the altering conditions around them.

## metamorphosis

When an organism goes through a major change in its body as it gets older. For example, a butterfly starts life as a caterpillar, before building a cocoon and finally emerging as the adult butterfly.

## molecule

The smallest unit of a chemical. Molecules can be very simple and made up of two atoms, such as the gas oxygen, or they can be very complex, as with DNA.

## notochord

A simple version of the backbone. It is a flexible rod that is found in some species and in the developing young of all vertebrates (animals with backbones).

## nucleus

The structure found inside a eukaryotic cell which houses its genetic material in the form of DNA.

## photosynthesis
The process by which plants use chlorophyll to capture the energy from sunlight, turning water and carbon dioxide into sugar and oxygen.

## producer
An organism that produces energy using sunlight.

## prokaryotic cell
A type of cell that does not have a nucleus to hold its genetic information.

## respiration
The process by which organisms produce energy, releasing carbon dioxide and water as a result.

## sexual reproduction
When two animals of the opposite sex produce young together.

## uterus
Part of the female reproductive system in mammals. It is where developing young grow before birth.

## vertebrate
An animal that has a backbone.

## virus
A type of organism that can only replicate inside another living being.

## species
A word used to describe organisms that can breed with each other and produce fertile offspring.

## Websites

**MORE INFO:**
**www.zsl.org**
The webiste of the Zoological Society of London. It contains information on conservation and the latest scientific studies on animal life.

**www.kids.nationalgeographic.com/kids**
Information on the latest scientific missions, and lots of games and facts about the natural world.

**www.nhm.ac.uk/kids-only**
The children's section of the Natural History Museum website is filled with games, facts and information on plants and animals, both living and extinct.

**MORE GRAPHICS:**
**www.visualinformation.info**
A website that contains a whole host of infographic material on subjects as diverse as natural history, science, sport and computer games.

**www.coolinfographics.com**
A collection of infographics and data visualisations from other online resources, magazines and newspapers

**www.dailyinfographic.com**
A comprehensive collection of infographics on an enormous range of topics that is updated every single day!

# INDEX

# ACKNOWLEDGEMENTS

First published in 2015 by Wayland
Copyright © Wayland 2015

Wayland, an imprint of
Hachette Children's Group
Part of Hodder & Stoughton
Carmelite House, 50 Victoria Embankment
London EC4Y 0DZ

All rights reserved.

Senior editor: Julia Adams
Produced by Tall Tree Ltd
Editor: Jon Richards
Designer: Ed Simkins
Consultant: Paola Oliveri

ISBN: 9780750289863

Dewey Number: 508-dc23

Printed in China

An Hachette UK company
www.hachette.co.uk
www.hachettechildrens.co.uk

The website addresses (URLs) included in this book were valid at the time of going to press. However, because of the nature of the Internet, it is possible that some addresses may have changed, or sites may have changed or closed down, since publication. While the author and Publisher regret any inconvenience this may cause the readers, no responsibility for any such changes can be accepted by either the author or the Publisher.